Healed, yet scarred

Aleena Khan

BookLeaf
Publishing

Presentation by *BookLeaf Publishing*

Web: www.bookleafpub.com

E-mail: info@bookleafpub.com

ISBN: 9789357745390

First edition 2023

DEDICATION

This book is dedicated to no one but myself :)

ACKNOWLEDGEMENT

Three cheers to all the beautiful souls around me who had my back always and to my father who pushed me into writing every day.
 My whole heart to that one stranger who turned out to be my bff for supporting me with anything I needed and always had my back no matter what.

Love,
Aleena

PREFACE

This book is a living, breathing book. Each word has been more than just an expression, more than just a feeling, more than just mere experience. It's an account of survival through the lows and highs of life.

 I request you to not just read the poems but feel every word and weave a string of imagination.

THE OVERTHINKER

Sometimes I consider myself Art,
Other times I just become
An overthinker.

THE SURVIVOR

Life feels so suffocating
These days.

It's difficult to breathe,
It's painful to pretend,
It's sad to live,
Like this..

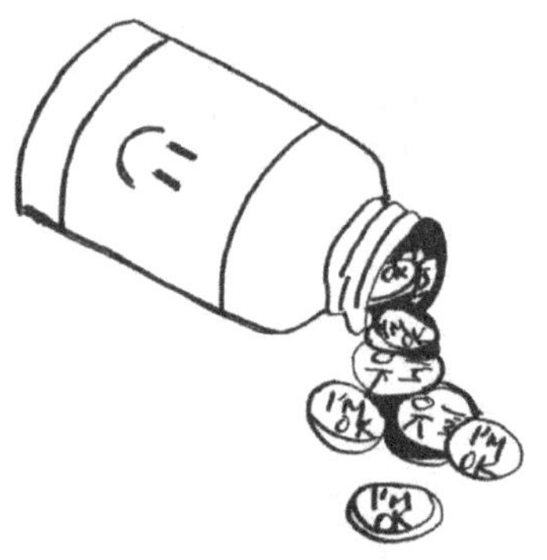

THE AVID READER

Some find their
comfort in music,
I like to lose myself
In stories portraying
Amazing characters and
I find solace in imagining myself
As the protagonist.

THE SCAR-BEARER

I healed,
Yet left scarred.
I guess I never heal completely..
Every scar, every pain,
Leaves me wanting to
Evaporate from this world,
Forever..

THE EXHAUSTED SOUL

I question my existence
Every night.
I recount all the heartbreaks
Of the day and realise
That this world,
Is not meant for me.

Maybe some other time,
Maybe some other world..

THE ANXIETY-RIDDEN

I'm angry at the world,
For breaking me
Little by little
Each day.

The nights are the worst..
I cry my eyes out
To sleep in peace,
Hoping that the mornings
Would calm my soul.

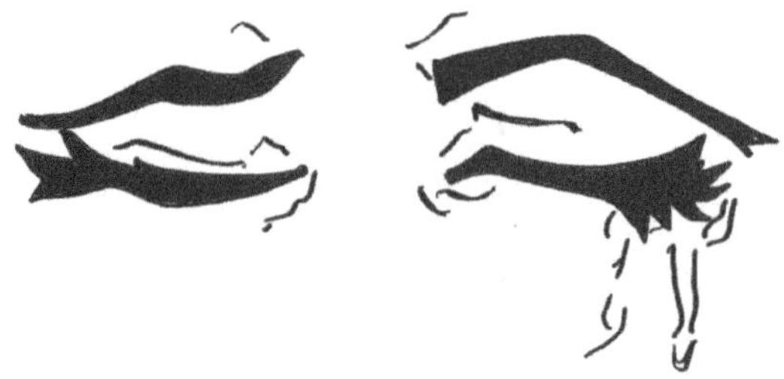

THE SUFFERER

Some days I feel so numb
That I sit in the shower
For hours and hours..
Hoping that the water
Will carry all my pain
And drain it down far away.

But that does not happen..
Instead, the cold water droplets
On my skin,
Make me feel vulnerable
To the inevitable pain.

THE HEALING HEART

I am happy
That I am healing.
Or at least what I though so..

[Sometimes, just a single person
Can make a huge difference
In your life].

I'm grateful for this day,
Today.

THE CAGED SOUL

I wish I could fly,
Like birds in the sky.
Doesn't matter low or high,
I just want to
Fly, fly and fly..

APOLOGY TO SELF

I feel so stupid right now,
When I look back at those times
I tried to harm my body and
Decided to end my life.

I now realise I can be so powerful,
And life can be so beautiful..
Now I have more reasons
To stay in this world
Than leave.

I am sorry
To my old self,
For breaking me each day,
Until yesterday..

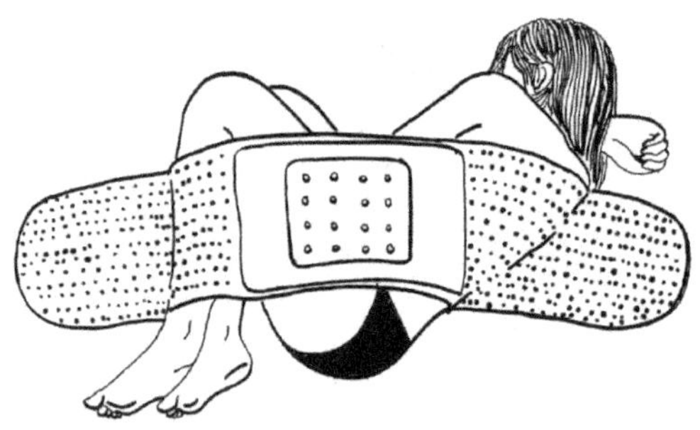

UNFAIR LIFE

Life has been so unfair
Most of the time..
And yet, we live like
There is no tomorrow.

It takes self clarity
And immense self-love,
To bloom like a wildflower again,
In order to enjoy life
To it's fullest.

THE DEATH OF ME

Something inside of me
Dies every night.
I become a black-hole of negativity
That sucks my sinister thought
And feelings of sadness,
All at once.
It makes me feel weak
And powerless,
And breaks every cell of my body
Until I panic and
Suffocate myself to Sleep..

THE WRONGDOER

I have been wronged,
Not once but
Many a times..
I find myself vulnerable
To the voices of truth,
As I can't stand being judged
Throughout my life.

THE BATTLE

It was time
For the warrior to rise,
As the soldier in me
Had died.

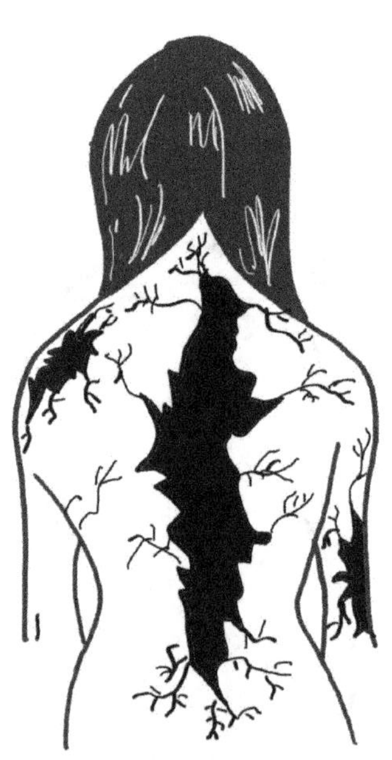

THE UNIQUE 'YOU'

I whispered to myself,
"Don't always strive
To be the best..
Give a chance to yourself
To be different
From the rest."

ENOUGH OF YOU!

You always needed
To pull me down,
I don't know why..
I could not tolerate anymore,
So I bid you Good-Bye!

FALSE BELIEFS

They mock me,
Make fun of me,
But I still don't back down.
I know I'm yet to be free
From this misery,
Which might turn me
Into an evil clown,
But I still don't back down.

Instead, I rise..
I rise higher and higher
To some place where no one
Can tell it's height.
It becomes wider and wider
When seen through my eyes.

People think I'm trash,
And yet in defence
I don't backlash.
Because I know,
That explaining to them
Won't be easy,
As their minds have become
Really greasy.

I don't want their words
To make me feel false pain,
As I know myself well enough

To believe their false
And treacherous blame.

They think that I can't recognise them
Through the masks they are wearing,
But they are unaware
Of the clown that I've played them.

I know each and everyone's
True root and stem.
But they still think,
That I don't know them.

Their words pierce
My soul sometimes,
But it's okay
As I don't keep any grudges.
My soul will settle through peace
Only when the brightest will I shine..
When I'll prove that I am capable
Of walking out calmly
Through any kind of mess.
Because now, I'm fed up
Of taking too much stress.

My heart says
I'll be there one day,
My soul believes
That I'm almost there.
And my mind tells me that
If I'll be productive enough

To utilise each second of mine,
I'm nonetheless there.

When my body is in unison
With my soul,
I have no reason to believe
The false faces around me,
Frowning at every achievement of mine,
With a questioning look
As if their hearts are made of coal.

But instead of punishing my soul,
I should let it set free,
In the calmness of the sea breeze
And nature's serenity.

THE HUMAN PANDEMONIUM

Kindness, is what you preach,
Understanding is what you crave.
Help, is what I need,
Until then I promise
That I'll be brave.

Love, is what I seek,
Pity is what you offer.
Envy, I should not leak,
As I don't wish to be jealous
Of him or her.

Healing, is what we require,
Scars are what we acquire.
Hurting, is a process so quick,
That you don't realise
Until one gets sick.

Slowly I'm learning
To sacrifice myself,
So that I can weave arbitrary wings,
After I offer you some help.

I don't keep ugliness in my heart,
Nor do I abuse you.

All I do is tear myself apart,
So that I disappear
Without leaving behind any hue.

I need a reason to smile,
I wish to freely breathe,
I want to walk miles,
And finally rest comfortably
Under the shades of neon,
And just read, read and read,
Till my eyes become weak.

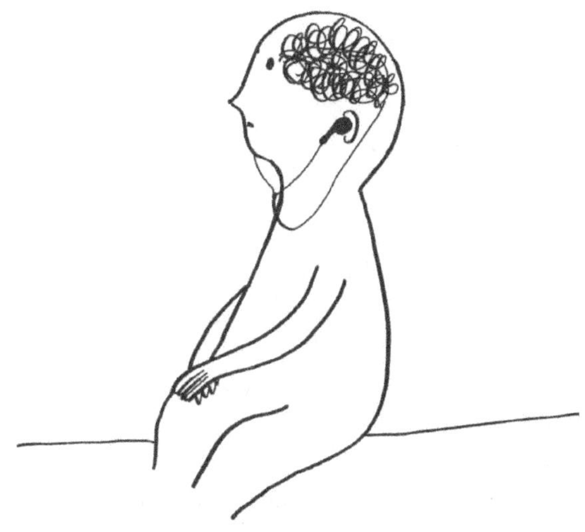

THERE'S BEAUTY IN IT

There's beauty
In being modest, shy and pious;
In speaking with a lowered voice,
And respecting other's opinions.

There's beauty
In helping the needy
And advising the troubled;
And there's beauty
I'm smiling at the hopeless.

There's beauty
In supporting the lonesome,
And in worrying
For the poverty-ridden.

There's beauty
In sharing your morsel
With the starving.
There's beauty,
In lending your wealth
To the needy.

There's beauty
In fighting your fears,
There's beauty,
In being calm towards the haughty.
Yes, there's beauty in it.

There's beauty
In standing against the corrupt,
In working day and night
To achieve your greatest height.

There's beauty
In treating the younger with compassion,
In healing the wounded,
In respecting the elders,
And in following rules.

There's beauty
In supporting the fragile,
In feeding the family,
In being kind to the worst,
And in quenching someone's thirst.
Yes, there's beauty in it.

There's beauty
In feeling numb,
In appreciating the dumb,
And in having fun under the sun.
There's beauty in it.
Yes, there's beauty in it.

A BAD DREAM

I was already in a void
The moment I went to bed,
The reality I wanted to avoid
With my satin pillow under my head.

I stood in the darkness all alone
With no one around for company.
I feared I might be disowned
By the emptiness as well,
Since I had been a wanderer for long.

Whichever side I tried to run,
I was stuck between
Darkness and emptiness.
I tried to stay shunned,
But the dingy darkness
Started to compress.

I cried, I shouted
But to no avail,
Stopped in silence,
As I realised the absence
Of any other living being
In the threatening ambiance.

Sweat rolled down my temple,
I was totally drenched
In the saline liquid.
I wished these memories
Would just erase,
And every sin I've ever committed,
I'd honestly admit.

But somebody really needed
To get me out of there,
So I could breathe in fresh air.
I felt I would die before
I could warn others to beware
Of this void,
This emptiness
And this loneliness,
Which could suck life
Out of anyone.

I feared I might be stuck here forever,
Or without leaving any clue,
I might just disappear.
But before I could disappear
Forever with just a gulp,
I found myself drowning in water,
While shouting for help.

And then I realised that I
Just escaped from a bad dream

With my mother's help.
Had she not poured water on me,
I might have forever stuck in there.

FAILURE OF A PARENT

A child fails,
When a parent fails
To understand them.

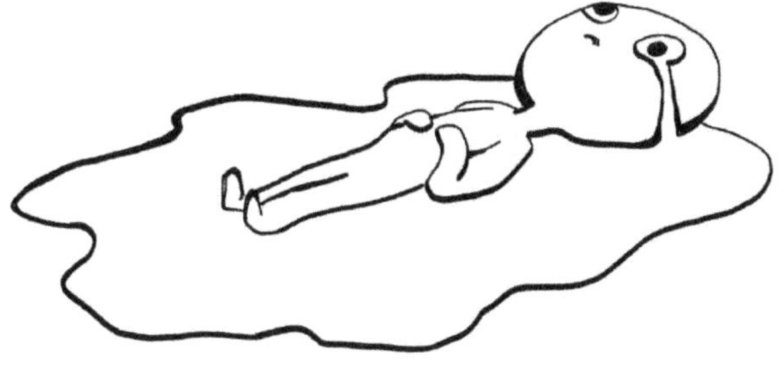